Hound for the Holidays

A Bark & Smile® Book

BY KIM LEVIN AND JOHN O'NEILL

**Andrews McMeel
Publishing, LLC**

Kansas City

09 TWP 10 9 8 7 6 5

ISBN-13: 978-0-7407-5567-5

ISBN-10: 0-7407-5567-6

Library of Congress Control Number: 2005923392

www.barkandsmile.com

To Charlie, the best hound around.

ACKNOWLEDGMENTS

Thank you to all of the hounds that appear in *Hound for the Holidays*. This book would not be possible without you.

Thanks to Dorothy O'Brien and the wonderful team at Andrews McMeel Publishing. We are happy that we have had such a long partnership with you. We'd also like to thank Jim Hutchison for his printing prowess. And lastly, to our favorite hound Charlie, thank you for your love and loyalty.

Happy Holidays!
K.L. and J.O.

This holiday season,
let's remember the things
that really matter.

\mathscr{F}amily reunions

Fireside chats

The Thanksgiving nap

Frosty mornings

Winter breezes

\mathcal{F}resh snow . . .

\mathcal{A}nd discovering it
for the first time

A trip to the big city

Window shopping

Thick sweaters

Long scarves

Warm mittens

Once-a-year couture

A little neighborhood caroling

Trimmed trees

Welcoming wreaths

*Y*our presence,
not your presents

38

Winter jaunts

*C*atching snowflakes on
your tongue . . .

Or on your nose

\mathcal{B}ody heat

\mathscr{F}rozen ponds

Buried treasure

50

Old-fashioned sleigh rides

Well-played

snowball fights

The last sip
of hot chocolate

56

\mathcal{S}low work days

\mathcal{S}anta's lap

Heading to grandma's house

Catching up

\mathcal{I}ndulging guilt-free

\mathcal{S}nowmen and candy canes

Big red bows

Stuffed stockings

New toys

The Christmas spirit

\mathcal{A} toast to the new year

Other Books by Kim Levin

Growing Up (with John O'Neill)
Dogma (with Erica Salmon)
Why We Love Cats
Why We Love Dogs
Why We Really Love Dogs
Dogs Are Funny
Dogs Love . . .

*Working Dogs: Tales from Animal
Planet's K-9 to 5 World*
Cattitude (with Christine Montaquila)
Erin Go Bark (with John O'Neill)
For the Love You Give (with John O'Neill)